Once Upon a Poem

The publishers would like to thank Susan Birkett, Kathleen Horning,
Andrew Medlar, Megan Schliesman, and Susan Stan for their invaluable help
in the selection process for this book.

First published in the United Kingdom in 2004 by The Chicken House,
2 Palmer Street, Frome, Somerset, BA11 1DS.

ISBN 0-439-77935-9

12 11 10 9 8 7 6 5 4 3 2 1   5 6 7 8 9 10/0
Printed in Mexico   49

First Scholastic paperback printing, April 2005

Book design by Ian Butterworth and Elizabeth Parisi

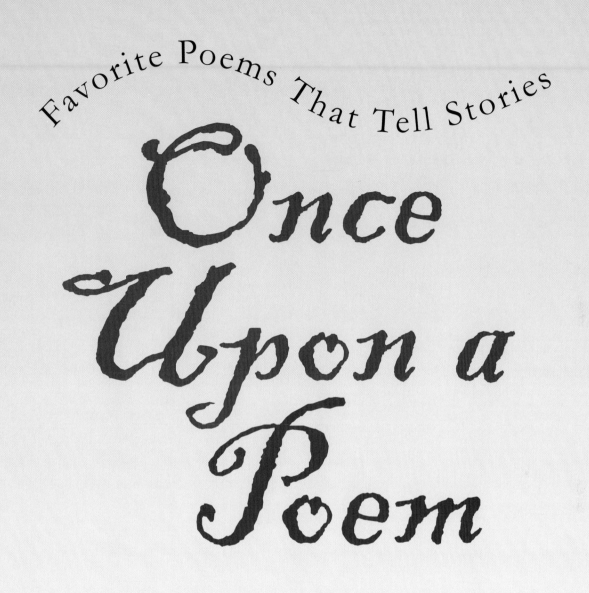

Favorite Poems That Tell Stories

Once Upon a Poem

Foreword by
KEVIN CROSSLEY-HOLLAND

Illustrated by

**PETER BAILEY, SIÂN BAILEY,
CAROL LAWSON, CHRIS MCEWAN**

SCHOLASTIC INC.
New York Toronto London Auckland Sydney
Mexico City New Delhi Hong Kong Buenos Aires

Contents

A Good Poem

I like a good poem
one with lots of fighting
in it. Blood, and the
clanging of armour. Poems

against Scotland are good,
and poems that defeat
the French with crossbows.
I don't like poems that

aren't about anything.
Sonnets are wet and
a waste of time.
Also poems that don't

know how to rhyme.
If I was a poem
I'd play football and
get picked for England.

By Roger McGough

Foreword

I thought I knew about burning blue cold. I mean, I've lived in northerly Minnesota, and that's where, in winter, you can snap off your moustache, if you've got one, or toss hot water into the air and watch the drops turn to ice before they fall to the ground.

But now I've met Sam McGee! He digs for gold in a place where stars tap-dance and huskies howl. And when Sam freezes to death, his chum has to keep going, he has to, because …

That's how these wonderful story-poems are. Because … and then … and then … because …

Some of them tell of challenges. Who can recapture the runaway colt that's worth a mint? How can Merlin find the snake's egg? And how is Bess to tell her lover in the thrilling, heartbreaking *The Highwayman* that soldiers in their redcoats are lying in wait for him?

If you eat nothing, you'll starve, and if you stuff yourself, you'll feel sick. Actions have consequences! Some of these story-poems are rather like that. Because a princess takes pity on a dragon "half the size of a football pitch," the grateful creature behaves in a most unexpected way. And because Noah's son is so very lazy, the Ark has to set sail without the sweet-scented, golden-hooved, most beautiful beast of all.

Then there are several complete surprises. In the astonishing *Jabberwocky*, Lewis Carroll describes a fight using dozens of words we've never even heard of but perfectly understand. And what about Goldilocks? "A nosey thieving little louse"? Roald Dahl asks us to look at the old story in a new way, and laugh. Magical *Wynken, Blynken, and Nod* by the American poet Eugene Field is a kind of sister-poem to Edward Lear's *The Owl and the Pussy-cat*, and they both make me realise how this book not only takes us on journeys to amazing places but into our own amazing heads and hearts.

These poems! Some gallop. They throb and they pulse. While others say in a quiet voice, "Hey, you! Heard this?" And something else: they all grab you by the collar. You're in at the deep end before you realise it.

Reading them, I've felt hot, cold, excited, brave, scared; they've made me laugh out loud, and one brought tears to my eyes; they've made me indignant and joyous; they've made me edge forward in my chair. They've shown me how we're all the same and, thank heavens, all completely different.

Each poem is championed by a famous storyteller—some of the world's best—and this is what they have in common: they all help us to see why these fifteen poems are also spellbinding stories.

We humans are hungry for stories. We began with *Humpty Dumpty* and *Hey diddle diddle* and rhymes like that and, although we keep hearing and reading new stories, we never forget the best old ones. That's why *Once Upon a Poem* is great for now and, happily, ever after!

Kevin Crossley-Holland

Jim who Ran Away from his Nurse,

and Was Eaten by a Lion

By Hilaire Belloc

"Belloc is one of my favourite poets for his wit, his understatement, and his profundity—but, perhaps most of all, for the lion called Ponto who ate Jim."

J. K. ROWLING

There was a boy whose name was Jim;
　　His friends were very good to him.
They gave him tea, and cakes, and jam,
　　And slices of delicious ham,
And chocolate with pink inside,
　　And little tricycles to ride,
And read him stories through and through,
　　And even took him to the Zoo—
But there it was the dreadful fate
　　Befell him, which I now relate.

You know—at least you *ought* to know,

For I have often told you so—

That children never are allowed

To leave their nurses in a crowd;

Now this was Jim's especial foible,

He ran away when he was able,

And on this inauspicious day

He slipped his hand and ran away!

He hadn't gone a yard when—

BANG!

With open jaws, a lion sprang,

And hungrily began to eat

The boy: beginning at his feet.

Now, just imagine how it feels

    When first your toes and then your heels,

And then by gradual degrees,

    Your shins and ankles, calves and knees,

Are slowly eaten, bit by bit.

    No wonder Jim detested it!

No wonder that he shouted "Hi!"

    The honest keeper heard his cry,

Though very fat he almost ran

    To help the little gentleman.

"Ponto!" he ordered as he came

    (For Ponto was the lion's name),

"Ponto!" he cried, with angry frown.

"Let go, Sir! Down, Sir!

    Put it down!"

The lion made a sudden stop,
    He let the dainty morsel drop,
And slunk reluctant to his cage,
    Snarling with disappointed rage.
But when he bent him over Jim,
    The honest keeper's eyes were dim.
The lion having reached his head,
    The miserable boy was dead!

When Nurse informed his parents, they
　　Were more concerned than I can say:—
His Mother, as she dried her eyes,
　　Said, "Well—it gives me no surprise,
He would not do as he was told!"
　　His Father, who was self-controlled,
Bade all the children round attend
　　To James's miserable end,

And always keep a-hold of Nurse
　　For fear of finding
　　　　something worse.

Paul Revere's Ride

By Henry Wadsworth Longfellow

"This poem begs to be read aloud.
I love the contrast in images of light and
dark, stillness and impending battle,
and above all, the pounding rhythm which
propels the story and echoes the
hoofbeats of Paul Revere's steed."

SHARON CREECH

Bedford

*L*isten, my children, and you shall hear
Of the midnight ride of Paul Revere,
On the eighteenth of April, in Seventy-five;
Hardly a man is now alive
Who remembers that famous day and year.

He said to his friend, "If the British march
By land or sea from the town tonight,
Hang a lantern aloft in the belfry arch
Of the North Church tower as a signal light—
One, if by land, and two, if by sea;
And I on the opposite shore will be,
Ready to ride and spread the alarm
Through every Middlesex village and farm,
For the country folk to be up and to arm."

Charlestown

Boston

18th April 1775

Then he said, "Good night!" and with muffled oar
Silently rowed to the Charlestown shore,
Just as the moon rose over the bay,
Where swinging wide at her moorings lay
The Somerset, British man-of-war;
A phantom ship, with each mast and spar
Across the moon like a prison bar,
And a huge black hulk, that was magnified
By its own reflection in the tide.

Meanwhile, his friend, through alley and street,
Wanders and watches with eager ears,
Till in the silence around him he hears
The muster of men at the barrack door,
The sound of arms, and the tramp of feet,
And the measured tread of the grenadiers,
Marching down to their boats on the shore.

Then he climbed the tower of the Old North Church,
By the wooden stairs, with stealthy tread,
To the belfry-chamber overhead,
And startled the pigeons from their perch
On the sombre rafters, that round him made
Masses and moving shapes of shade—
By the trembling ladder, steep and tall,
To the highest window in the wall,
Where he paused to listen and look down
A moment on the roofs of the town,
And the moonlight flowing over all.

21

Beneath, in the churchyard, lay the dead,
In their night-encampment on the hill,
Wrapped in silence so deep and still
That he could hear, like a sentinel's tread,
The watchful night-wind, as it went
Creeping along from tent to tent,
And seeming to whisper, "All is well!"
A moment only he feels the spell
Of the place and the hour, and the secret dread
Of the lonely belfry and the dead;
For suddenly all his thoughts are bent
On a shadowy something far away,
Where the river widens to meet the bay—
A line of black that bends and floats
On the rising tide, like a bridge of boats.

Meanwhile, impatient to mount and ride,
Booted and spurred, with a heavy stride
On the opposite shore walked Paul Revere.
Now he patted his horse's side,
Now gazed at the landscape far and near,
Then, impetuous, stamped the earth,
And turned and tightened his saddle-girth;
But mostly he watched with eager search
The belfry-tower of the Old North Church,

As it rose above the graves on the hill,
Lonely and spectral and sombre and still.
And lo! as he looks, on the belfry's height
A glimmer, and then a gleam of light!
He springs to the saddle, the bridle he turns,
But lingers and gazes, till full on his sight
A second lamp in the belfry burns!

A hurry of hoofs in a village street,
A shape in the moonlight, a bulk in the dark,
And beneath, from the pebbles, in passing, a spark
Struck out by a steed flying fearless and fleet;
That was all! And yet, through the gloom and the light
The fate of a nation was riding that night;
And the spark struck out by that steed in his flight,
Kindled the land into flame with its heat.

He has left the village and mounted the steep,
And beneath him, tranquil and broad and deep,
Is the Mystic, meeting the ocean tides;
And under the alders, that skirt its edge,
Now soft on the sand, now loud on the ledge,
Is heard the tramp of his steed as he rides.

It was twelve by the village clock,
When he crossed the bridge into Medford town.
He heard the crowing of the cock,
And the barking of the farmer's dog,
And felt the damp of the river fog,
That rises after the sun goes down.

It was one by the village clock,
When he galloped into Lexington.
He saw the gilded weathercock
Swim in the moonlight as he passed,
And the meeting-house windows, blank and bare,
Gaze at him with a spectral glare,
As if they already stood aghast
At the bloody work they would look upon.

It was two by the village clock,
When he came to the bridge in Concord town.
He heard the bleating of the flock,
And the twitter of birds among the trees,
And felt the breath of the morning breeze
Blowing over the meadows brown.
And one was safe and asleep in his bed
Who at the bridge would be first to fall,
Who that day would by lying dead,
Pierced by a British musket-ball.

You know the rest. In the books you have read,
How the British Regulars fired and fled—
How the farmers gave them ball for ball,
From behind each fence and farmyard wall,
Chasing the redcoats down the lane,
Then crossing the fields to emerge again
Under the trees at the turn of the road,
And only pausing to fire and load.

So through the night rode Paul Revere;
And so through the night went his cry of alarm
To every Middlesex village and farm—
A cry of defiance, and not of fear,
A voice in the darkness, a knock at the door,
And a word that shall echo for evermore!
For, borne on the night-wind of the past,
Through all our history, to the last,
In the hour of darkness and peril and need,
The people will waken and listen to hear
The hurrying hoofbeats of that steed,
And the midnight message of Paul Revere.

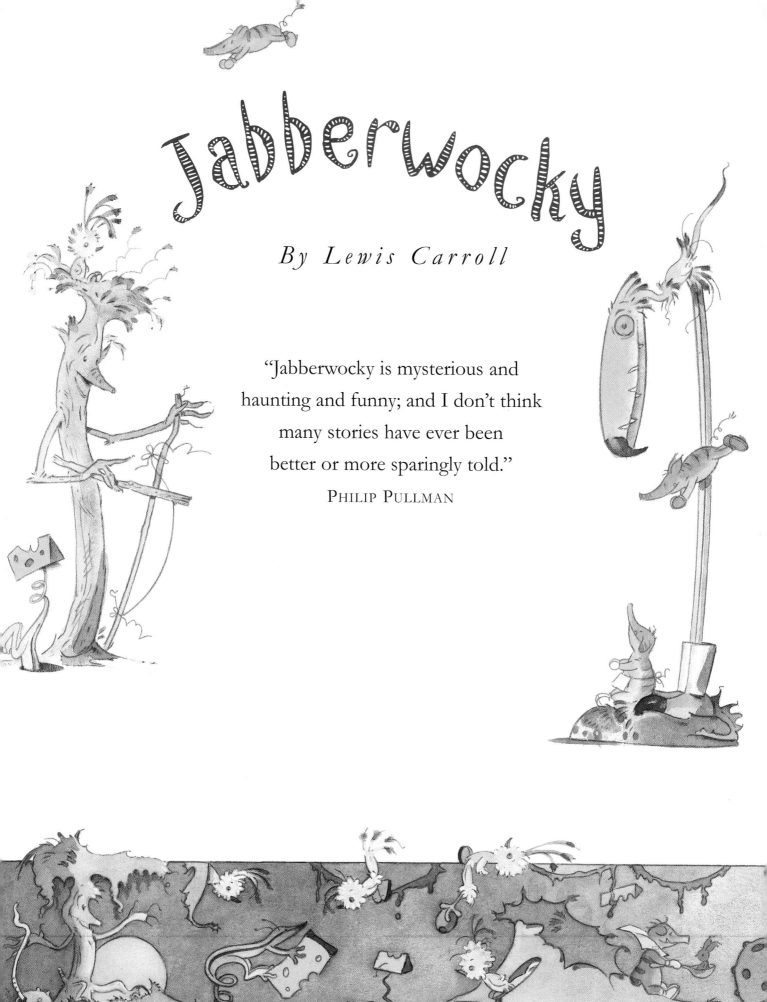

Jabberwocky

By Lewis Carroll

"Jabberwocky is mysterious and
haunting and funny; and I don't think
many stories have ever been
better or more sparingly told."
PHILIP PULLMAN

'Twas brillig, and the slithy toves
Did gyre and gimble in the wabe:
All mimsy were the borogoves,
    And the mome raths outgrabe.

"Beware the Jabberwock, my son!
    The jaws that bite, the claws that catch!
Beware the Jubjub bird, and shun
    The frumious Bandersnatch!"

He took his vorpal sword in hand:
  Long time the manxome foe he sought—
So rested he by the Tumtum tree,
  And stood awhile in thought.

And as in uffish thought he stood,
  The Jabberwock, with eyes of flame,
Came whiffling through the tulgey wood,

And burbled as it came!

One, two! One, two!

And through and through

The vorpal blade went snicker-snack!

He left it dead, and with its head

He went **galumphing** back.

"And hast thou slain the Jabberwock?
  Come to my arms, my beamish boy!
O frabjous day! Callooh! Callay!"
  He chortled in his joy.

'Twas brillig, and the slithy toves
Did gyre and gimble in the wabe:
All mimsy were the borogoves,
And the mome raths outgrabe.

Merlin and the

By Leslie Norris

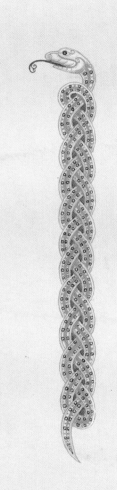

"How is a young man called Merlin able
to become the greatest magician of all—and
how does his old dog help him?
Leslie Norris casts his own magical spell
with answers simple and yet mysterious,
age-old yet leaping and new."
KEVIN CROSSLEY-HOLLAND

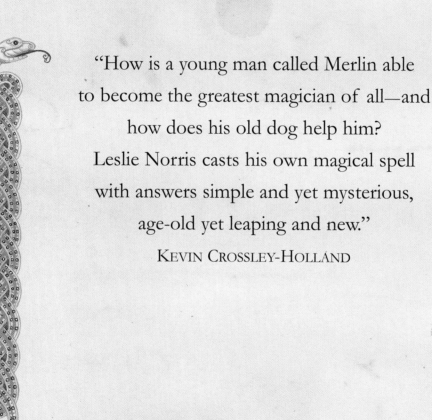

Snake's Egg

*A*ll night the tall young man
Reads in his book of spells,
Learning the stratagems,
The chants and diagrams,
The words to serve him well
When he's the world's magician.

But he needs the snake's egg.

The night is thick as soot,

The dark wind's at rest,

The fire's low in the grate.

The black dog stirs and moans

Where he lies at Merlin's feet.

Dreams trouble his sleep.

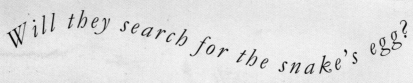

Will they search for the snake's egg?

For the purest of magic

Four things must be found:

Green cress from the river,

Gold herbs from the ground,

The top twig of the high oak;

And the snake's round, white egg.

Will they find the snake's egg?

Early, before white dawn
  Disturbs the sleeping world,
Merlin is on his way
  To the forbidden wood.
Glain, the old black dog,
  Walks where his master walked.

They go for the snake's egg.

Glain, are yours the eyes
　　To see where the leaf turns?
To know the small, dark hole
　　Where the mouse's eye burns?
Will your ears pick up the sound
　　Of the mole's breath underground?

Can you find the snake's egg?

Merlin stands at the water's edge,
　　At the river's flood.
He stands in the salmon's scales,
　　His blood is the salmon's blood.
He swims in the slanting stream,
　　In the white foam a whiter gleam.

He has pulled the green cresses.

Merlin stands in the wide field
  Where the small creatures hide.
His long, straight limbs are lost,
  He is changed to a spider.
He crawls on awkward joints, his head
  Moves from side to side.

He has cropped the gold herbs.

Merlin stands beneath the oak.

Feathers sprout from his arms.

His nose is an owl's hooked nose,

His voice one of night's alarms,

His eyes are the owl's round eyes.

Silent and soft he flies.

He has brought down the top twig.

But Glain in the troubled wood
  Steadfastly searches.
The day's last light leans in
  Under the bushes.
And there, like a little moon,
  Pale, round and shining,

He has found the snake's egg.

The Man From Snowy River

By A.B. "Banjo" Paterson

"Whenever I feel slight and weedy, I
think of this poem. I like stories where
underdogs (or horses) get to be heroes.
Thanks, Banjo, you're a tonic."
MORRIS GLEITZMAN

There was movement at the station, for the word had passed around
    That the colt from old Regret had got away,
And had joined the wild bush horses—he was worth a thousand pound,
    So all the cracks had gathered to the fray.
All the tried and noted riders from the stations near and far
    Had mustered at the homestead overnight,
For the bushmen love hard riding where the wild bush horses are,
    And the stock-horse snuffs the battle with delight.

There was Harrison, who made his pile when Pardon won the cup,
    The old man with his hair as white as snow;
But few could ride beside him when his blood was fairly up—
    He would go wherever horse and man could go.
And Clancy of the Overflow came down to lend a hand,
    No better horseman ever held the reins;
For never horse could throw him while the saddle-girths would stand—
    He learnt to ride while droving on the plains.

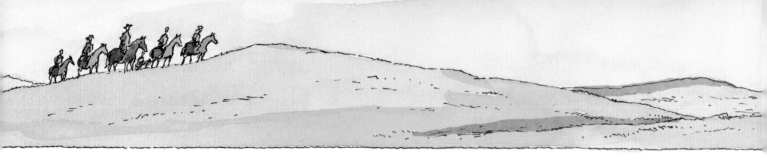

And one was there, a stripling on a small and weedy beast;
    He was something like a racehorse undersized,
With a touch of Timor pony—three parts thoroughbred at least—
    And such as are by mountain horsemen prized.
He was hard and tough and wiry—just the sort that won't say die—
    There was courage in his quick impatient tread;
And he bore the badge of gameness in his bright and fiery eye,
    And the proud and lofty carriage of his head.

But still so slight and weedy, one would doubt his power to stay,
    And the old man said, "That horse will never do
For a long and tiring gallop—lad, you'd better stop away,
    Those hills are far too rough for such as you."
So he waited, sad and wistful—only Clancy stood his friend—
    "I think we ought to let him come," he said;
"I warrant he'll be with us when he's wanted at the end,
    For both his horse and he are mountain bred.

"He hails from Snowy River, up by Kosciusko's side,
    Where the hills are twice as steep and twice as rough;
Where a horse's hoofs strike firelight from the flint stones every stride,
    The man that holds his own is good enough.

And the Snowy River riders on the mountains make their home,
　　Where the river runs those giant hills between;
I have seen full many horsemen since I first commenced to roam,
　　But nowhere yet such horsemen have I seen."

So he went; they found the horses by the big mimosa clump,
　　They raced away towards the mountain's brow,
And the old man gave his orders, "Boys, go at them from the jump,
　　No use to try for fancy riding now.
And, Clancy, you must wheel them, try and wheel them to the right.
　　Ride boldly, lad, and never fear the spills,
For never yet was rider that could keep the mob in sight,
　　If once they gain the shelter of those hills."

So Clancy rode to wheel them—he was racing on the wing
    Where the best and boldest riders take their place,
And he raced his stock-horse past them, and he made the ranges ring
    With the stockwhip, as he met them face to face.
Then they halted for a moment, while he swung the dreaded lash,
    But they saw their well-loved mountain full in view,
And they charged beneath the stockwhip with a sharp and sudden dash,
    And off into the mountain scrub they flew.

Then fast the horsemen followed, where the gorges deep and black
  Resounded to the thunder of their tread,
And the stockwhips woke the echoes, and they fiercely answered back
  From cliffs and crags that beetled overhead.
And upward, ever upward, the wild horses held their way,
  Where mountain ash and kurrajong grew wide;
And the old man muttered fiercely, "We may bid the mob good day,
  No man can hold them down the other side."

When they reached the mountain's summit, even Clancy took a pull—
  It well might make the boldest hold their breath;
The wild hop scrub grew thickly, and the hidden ground was full
  Of wombat holes, and any slip was death.
But the man from Snowy River let the pony have his head,
  And he swung his stockwhip round and gave a cheer,
And he raced him down the mountain like a torrent down its bed,
  While the others stood and watched in very fear.

He sent the flint-stones flying, but the pony kept his feet,
    He cleared the fallen timber in his stride,
And the man from Snowy River never shifted in his seat—
    It was grand to see that mountain horseman ride.
Through the stringy barks and saplings, on the rough and broken ground,
    Down the hillside at a racing pace he went;
And he never drew the bridle till he landed safe and sound
    At the bottom of that terrible descent.

He was right among the horses as they climbed the farther hill,
    And the watchers on the mountain, standing mute,
Saw him ply the stockwhip fiercely; he was right among them still,
    As he raced across the clearing in pursuit.
Then they lost him for a moment, where two mountain gullies met
    In the ranges—but a final glimpse reveals
On a dim and distant hillside the wild horses racing yet,
    With the man from Snowy River at their heels.

And he ran them single-handed till their sides were white with foam;

    He followed like a bloodhound on their track,

Till they halted, cowed and beaten; then he turned their heads for home,

    And alone and unassisted brought them back.

But his hardy mountain pony he could scarcely raise a trot,

    He was blood from hip to shoulder from the spur;

But his pluck was still undaunted, and his courage fiery hot,

    For never yet was mountain horse a cur.

And down by Kosciusko, where the pine-clad ridges raise

    Their torn and rugged battlements on high,

Where the air is clear as crystal, and the white stars fairly blaze

    At midnight in the cold and frosty sky,

And where around the Overflow the reed-beds sweep and sway

    To the breezes, and the rolling plains are wide,

The man from Snowy River is a household word today,

    And the stockmen tell the story of his ride.

A Visit from St. Nicholas

By Clement Clarke Moore

"Packed with vivid realistic detail, written in fast, compelling rhythms, this poem grabs you from the very start, and I, for one, can't think of breaking free until its tale is told."

DAVID ALMOND

'Twas the night before Christmas, when all through the house
Not a creature was stirring, not even a mouse;
   The stockings were hung by the chimney with care,
In hopes that St. Nicholas soon would be there;
   The children were nestled all snug in their beds;
While visions of sugar-plums danced in their heads;
   And mamma in her 'kerchief, and I in my cap,
Had just settled our brains for a long winter's nap—

When out on the lawn there arose such a clatter,

 I sprang from my bed to see what was the matter.

Away to the window I flew like a flash,

 Tore open the shutters, and threw up the sash.

The moon, on the breast of the new-fallen snow,

 Gave the luster of midday to objects below;

When, what to my wondering eyes should appear,

 But a miniature sleigh and eight tiny reindeer,

With a little old driver, so lively and quick,

 I knew in a moment it must be St. Nick.

More rapid than eagles his coursers they came,

 And he whistled, and shouted, and called them by name;

"Now, DASHER! now, DANCER! now, PRANCER and VIXEN!

    On, COMET! on, CUPID! on, DONDER and BLITZEN!

To the top of the porch! to the top of the wall!

    Now dash away! dash away! dash away all!"

As dry leaves that before the wild hurricane fly,

    When they meet with an obstacle, mount to the sky;

So up to the house-top the coursers they flew

    With the sleigh full of toys, and St. Nicholas too.

And then, in a twinkling, I heard on the roof

    The prancing and pawing of each little hoof—

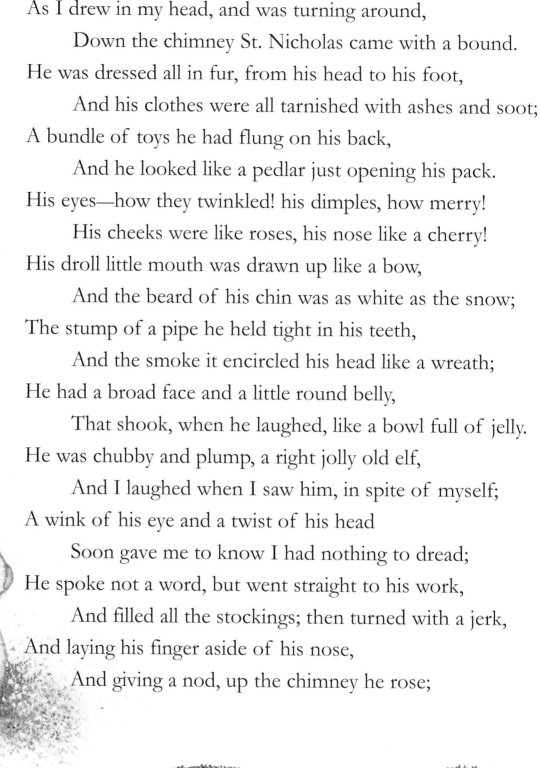

As I drew in my head, and was turning around,

    Down the chimney St. Nicholas came with a bound.

He was dressed all in fur, from his head to his foot,

    And his clothes were all tarnished with ashes and soot;

A bundle of toys he had flung on his back,

    And he looked like a pedlar just opening his pack.

His eyes—how they twinkled! his dimples, how merry!

    His cheeks were like roses, his nose like a cherry!

His droll little mouth was drawn up like a bow,

    And the beard of his chin was as white as the snow;

The stump of a pipe he held tight in his teeth,

    And the smoke it encircled his head like a wreath;

He had a broad face and a little round belly,

    That shook, when he laughed, like a bowl full of jelly.

He was chubby and plump, a right jolly old elf,

    And I laughed when I saw him, in spite of myself;

A wink of his eye and a twist of his head

    Soon gave me to know I had nothing to dread;

He spoke not a word, but went straight to his work,

    And filled all the stockings; then turned with a jerk,

And laying his finger aside of his nose,

    And giving a nod, up the chimney he rose;

He sprang to his sleigh, to his team gave a whistle,
   And away they all flew like the down of a thistle.
But I heard him exclaim, ere he drove out of sight,

"HAPPY CHRISTMAS TO ALL, AND TO ALL A GOOD NIGHT!"

BRAVE BOY RAP

By Tony Mitton

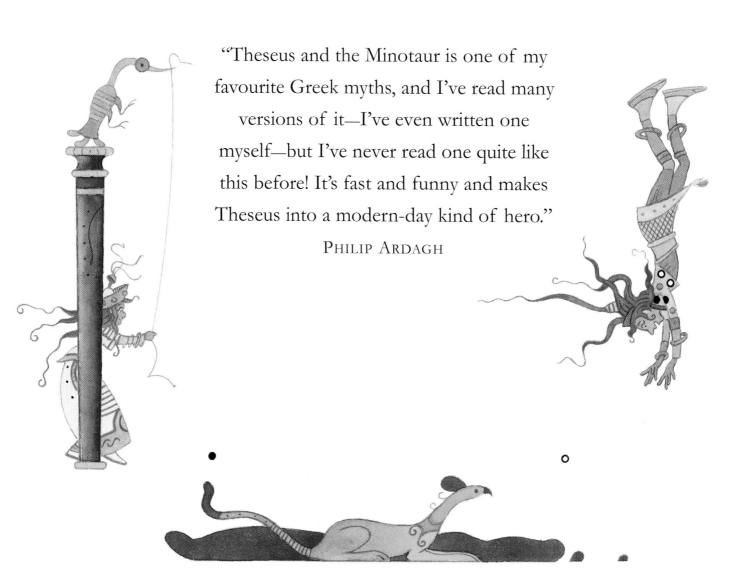

"Theseus and the Minotaur is one of my favourite Greek myths, and I've read many versions of it—I've even written one myself—but I've never read one quite like this before! It's fast and funny and makes Theseus into a modern-day kind of hero."

PHILIP ARDAGH

Prince Theseus
was a brave young lad.
Big bullies made him
boiling mad.
So when he heard
about a beast
whose horrid habit
was to feast
on gals 'n' guys,
he frowned, "OK!"
and went to fight it
that same day.

This beast was called
the Minotaur.
It lived beneath
a palace floor
upon the nearby
Isle of Crete.
It stomped about
on hooves, not feet.

Its head and shoulders
were all bull.
It also had
a tail to pull.
The rest of it
was muscle guy,
a real meanie—
true! No lie!

It spent long nights
and boring days
just sulking in
a prison maze.

Except at feed times,
when its meals
were sent to it
with shrieks and squeals.

These meals were children
sent to be
the monster's breakfast,
lunch and tea!

Prince Theseus strode up
from the shore
and knocked upon
the palace door.

He told the king
he'd come as lunch
for hungry Minotaur
to munch.
The king took Theseus
along,
then rang the monster's
dinner gong.

The king slipped off.
But just before
our hero entered
the Minotaur's door
the princess
(what a sassy girl!)
came sidling up
in quite a whirl.

She gazed at him
and boldly said,
"I hope you'll knock
that monster dead.

Now, for the maze,
you'll need this thread.
Just tie it here.
When it's unravelled
the thread will tell you
where you've travelled.
You'll find me waiting
in my coat.

I'll take you safely
to your boat.

My dad would kill me
if he knew
that I was down here
helping you.
But I can't stand
to see kids eaten.
It's time my dad
and his beast were beaten.

So take me with you
when you go.
I think you're gorgeous.
Good luck. Yo!"

Brave Theseus wound
his way along.
And soon he smelled
a monstrous pong.
"Phew! That must
be the Minotaur …"

He heard a swish,
a thump, a roar.
And then he saw
a big bull's head.
"You ugly dork!"
our brave prince said.

He kicked its butt
and yanked its tail.
He tweaked its ears
and made it wail.
He cried, "I'm not
a snack to scoff,"
then grabbed its horns
and pulled them off.

60

The rest is rather
quick to tell.
He sent the monster
straight to hell.

Then back he went
along the thread.
"Oh, well done, dude!"
the princess said.
They tip-toed lightly
to the shore,
and sailed away
for evermore.

61

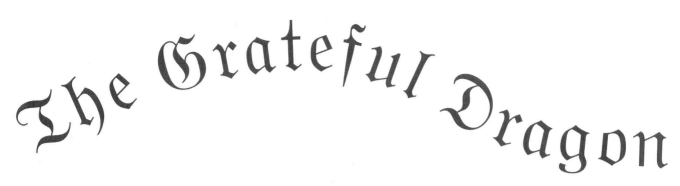

The Grateful Dragon

By Raymond Wilson

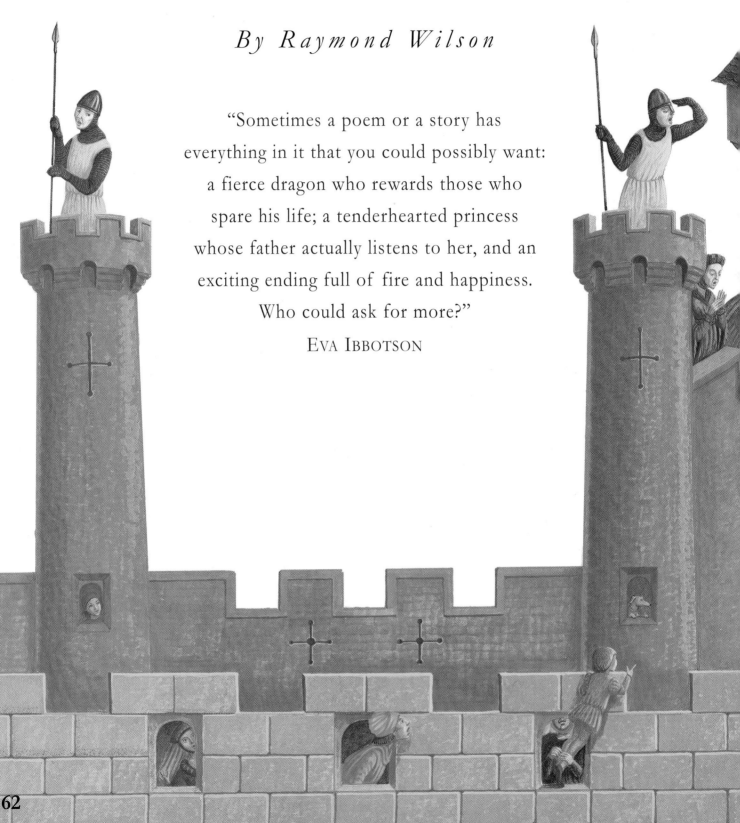

"Sometimes a poem or a story has
everything in it that you could possibly want:
a fierce dragon who rewards those who
spare his life; a tenderhearted princess
whose father actually listens to her, and an
exciting ending full of fire and happiness.
Who could ask for more?"

Eva Ibbotson

A dragon crawled to the castle door
    and everyone inside
looked down on it from the castle walls,
    curious but terrified.

It was half the size of a football pitch,
    bright green, with spots of red,
but it hadn't the strength to lash its tail
    and lay there, as if dead.

The Winter had turned the woods to iron,
the snow was deep as a house;
there wasn't a blade of grass to be seen
nor a skinny harvest mouse.

"It's starving!" the King cried. "Now's our chance!"—
looking down from the castle wall—
"Bring lances and crossbows and arrows
and let's kill it, once for all."

The dragon was too weak to move
more than an eyelid, and yet
the Princess saw a tear form there and it
moved her heart with regret.

"Please spare the dragon!" the Princess begged.
"Put out some bundles of hay.
Once it's grown strong from eating it will
harmlessly go away."

The King looked hard in his daughter's face
and saw how much she cared,
then nodded that they should do as she asked,
and so the dragon was spared.

Next Autumn brought enemy soldiers.
The King and his subjects shut
themselves in the castle, and there they starved
while the harvest stayed uncut.

The Princess wept on the castle wall
when suddenly there came

in a whirlwind of thunder and fury
the dragon, spouting flame.

The enemy soldiers ran off in fright
and never again were seen;
and the people came out of the castle
and gathered the harvest in.

"This poem takes you to another place
and another time with the very first
words, and it doesn't let you go till you
have read the last one. It is so vivid
that you feel the wind in your hair and
the rifle at your breast. You hear
the horse gallop through the night
(you have the feeling you'll hear it forever)
and you see the highwayman in your yard.
It is pure magic—it's storytelling!"

CORNELIA FUNKE

The Highwayman

By Alfred Noyes

The wind was a torrent of darkness among the gusty trees,
The moon was a ghostly galleon tossed upon cloudy seas,
The road was a ribbon of moonlight over the purple moor,
And the highwayman came riding—
    Riding—riding—
The highwayman came riding, up to the old inn-door.

He'd a French cocked-hat on his forehead, a bunch of lace at his chin,
A coat of the claret velvet, and breeches of brown doeskin:
They fitted with never a wrinkle; his boots were up to the thigh!
And he rode with a jewelled twinkle,
    His pistol butts a-twinkle,
His rapier hilt a-twinkle, under the jewelled sky.

Over the cobbles he clattered and clashed in the dark inn-yard,
And he tapped with his whip on the shutters, but all was locked and barred:
He whistled a tune to the window, and who should be waiting there
But the landlord's black-eyed daughter,
    Bess, the landlord's daughter,
Plaiting a dark red love-knot into her long black hair.

And dark in the dark old inn-yard a stable-wicket creaked
Where Tim, the ostler, listened; his face was white and peaked,
His eyes were hollows of madness, his hair like mouldy hay;
But he loved the landlord's daughter,
      The landlord's red-lipped daughter:
Dumb as a dog he listened, and he heard the robber say—

"One kiss, my bonny sweetheart, I'm after a prize tonight,
But I shall be back with the yellow gold before the morning light.
Yet if they press me sharply, and harry me through the day,
Then look for me by moonlight,
      Watch for me by moonlight:
I'll come to thee by moonlight, though Hell should bar the way."

He rose upright in the stirrups, he scarce could reach her hand;
But she loosened her hair i' the casement! His face burnt like a brand
As the black cascade of perfume came tumbling over his breast;
And he kissed its waves in the moonlight,
(Oh, sweet black waves in the moonlight)
Then he tugged at his reins in the moonlight, and galloped away to the West.

He did not come in the dawning; he did not come at noon;

And out of the tawny sunset, before the rise o' the moon,

When the road was a gypsy's ribbon, looping the purple moor,

A red-coat troop came marching—

Marching—marching—

King George's men came marching, up to the old inn-door.

They said no word to the landlord, they drank his ale instead;

But they gagged his daughter and bound her to the foot of her narrow bed.

Two of them knelt at her casement, with muskets at the side!

There was death at every window;

And Hell at one dark window;

For Bess could see, through her casement, the road that *he* would ride.

They had tied her up to attention, with many a sniggering jest:
They had bound a musket beside her, with the barrel beneath her breast!
"Now keep good watch!" and they kissed her.
         She heard the dead man say—

Look for me by moonlight;
         Watch for me by moonlight;

I'll come to thee by moonlight, though Hell should bar the way!

She twisted her hands behind her; but all the knots held good!
She writhed her hands till her fingers were wet with sweat or blood!
They stretched and strained in the darkness, and the hours crawled by
   like years;
Till, now, on the stroke of midnight,
         Cold, on the stroke of midnight,
The tip of one finger touched it! The trigger at least was hers!

The tip of one finger touched it; she strove no more for the rest!
Up, she stood up to attention, with the barrel beneath her breast,
She would not risk their hearing: she would not strive again;
For the road lay bare in the moonlight,
         Blank and bare in the moonight;
And the blood of her veins in the moonlight, throbbed to her
   Love's refrain.

Tlot-tlot, tlot-tlot! Had they heard it? The horse-hoofs ringing clear—
Tlot-tlot, tlot-tlot, in the distance? Were they deaf that they did not hear?
Down the ribbon of moonlight, over the brow of the hill,
The highwayman came riding,
>>## Riding, riding!
The red-coats looked to their priming! She stood up straight and still!

Tlot-tlot, in the frosty silence! *Tlot-tlot* in the echoing night!
Nearer he came and nearer! Her face was like a light!
Her eyes grew wide for a moment; she drew one last deep breath,
Then her finger moved in the moonlight,
>>## Her musket shattered the moonlight,
Shattered her breast in the moonlight and warned him—with her death.

He turned; he spurred him Westward; he did not know who stood
Bowed with her head o'er the musket, drenched with her own red blood!
Not till the dawn he heard it, and slowly blanched to hear
How Bess, the landlord's daughter,
The landlord's black-eyed daughter,
Had watched for her Love in the moonlight; and died in the darkness there.

Back, he spurred like a madman, shrieking a curse to the sky,
With the white road smoking behind him, and his rapier brandished high!
Blood-red were his spurs i' the golden noon; wine-red was his velvet coat;
When they shot him down on the highway,
Down like a dog on the highway,
And he lay in his blood on the highway, with the bunch of lace at his throat.

And still a winter's night, they say, when the wind is in the trees,
When the moon is a ghostly galleon tossed upon cloudy seas,
When the road is a ribbon of moonlight over the purple moor,
A highwayman comes riding—
Riding—riding—
A highwayman comes riding, up to the old inn-door.

Over the cobbles he clatters and clangs in the dark inn-yard;
And he taps with his whip on the shutters, but all is locked and barred:
He whistles a tune to the window, and who should be waiting there
But the landlord's black-eyed daughter,

Bess, the landlord's daughter,
Plaiting a dark red love-knot into her long black hair.

The Late Passenger

By C.S. Lewis

"A poem that captures the awe and wonder
of an ancient story and transports you
through time to a rainy night long, long ago."

The sky was low, the sounding rain was falling dense and dark,
And Noah's sons were standing at the window of the Ark.

The beasts were in, but Japhet said, "I see one creature more
Belated and unmated there come knocking at the door."

"Well let him knock," said Ham, "Or let him drown or learn to swim.
We're overcrowded as it is; we've got no room for him."

"And yet it knocks, how terribly it knocks," said Shem, "Its feet
Are hard as horn—but oh the air that comes from it is sweet."

"Now hush," said Ham, "You'll waken Dad, and once he comes to see
What's at the door, it's sure to mean more work for you and me."

Noah's voice came roaring from the darkness down below,
"Some animal is knocking. Take it in before we go."

Ham shouted back, and savagely he nudged the other two,
"That's only Japhet knocking down a brad-nail in his shoe."

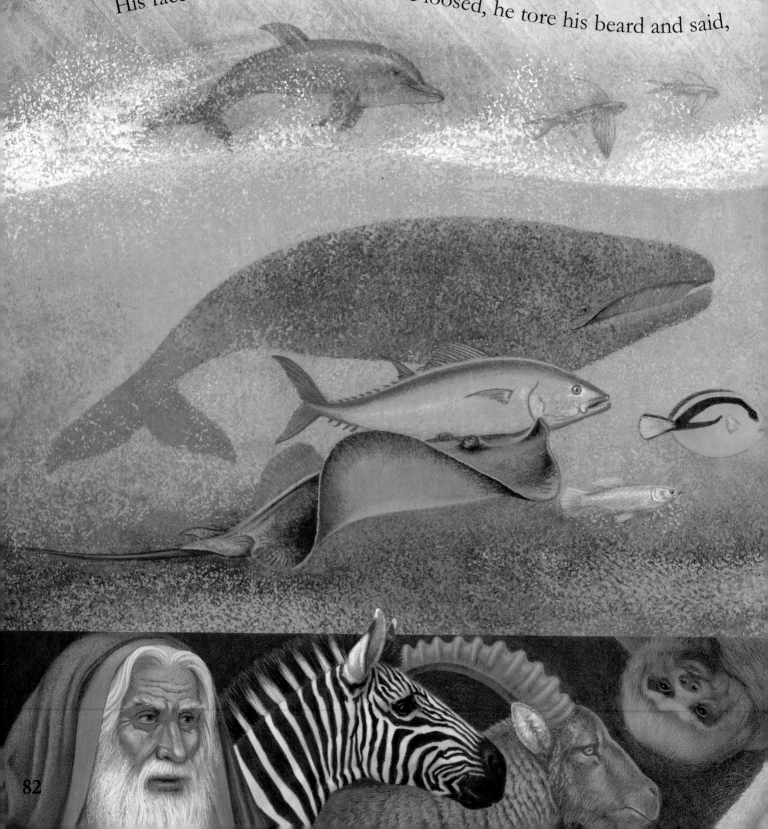

Said Noah, "Boys, I hear a noise that's like a horse's hoof."
Said Ham, "Why, that's the dreadful rain that drums upon the roof."

Noah tumbled up on deck and out he put his head;
His face went grey, his knees were loosed, he tore his beard and said,

"Look, look! It would not wait. It turns away. It takes its flight.
Fine work you've made of it, my sons, between you all tonight!

"Even if I could outrun it now, it would not turn again
—Not now. Our great discourtesy has earned its high disdain.

84

"Oh noble and unmated beast, my sons were all unkind;
In such a night what stable and what manger will you find?

"Oh golden hoofs, oh cataracts of mane, oh nostrils wide
With indignation! Oh the neck wave-arched, the lovely pride!

"Oh long shall be the furrows ploughed across the hearts of men
Before it comes to stable and to manger once again,

"And dark and crooked all the ways in which our race shall walk,
And shrivelled all their manhood like a flower with broken stalk,

"And all the world, oh Ham, may curse the hour when you were born;
Because of you the Ark must sail without the Unicorn."

Goldilocks and the

By Roald Dahl

"*Goldilocks* by Roald Dahl turns the fairy
story on its ear, and provides a new
suitably gruesome Dahlesque finale. At
last, justice is served. Literally."

EOIN COLFER

Three Bears

This famous wicked little tale
Should never have been put on sale.
It is a mystery to me
Why loving parents cannot see
That this is actually a book
About a brazen little crook.
Had I the chance I wouldn't fail
To clap young Goldilocks in jail.
Now just imagine how *you'd* feel
If you had cooked a lovely meal,
Delicious porridge, steaming hot,
Fresh coffee in the coffee-pot,
With maybe toast and marmalade,
The table beautifully laid,
One place for you and one for dad,
Another for your little lad.

Then dad cries, "Golly-gosh! Gee-whizz!
"Oh cripes! How hot this porridge is!

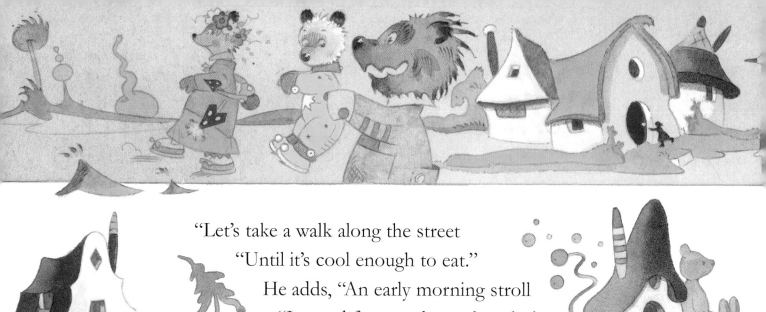

"Let's take a walk along the street
"Until it's cool enough to eat."
He adds, "An early morning stroll
"Is good for people on the whole.
"It makes your appetite improve
"It also helps your bowels to move."
No proper wife would dare to question
Such a sensible suggestion,
Above all not at breakfast-time
When men are seldom at their prime.
No sooner are you down the road
Than Goldilocks, that little toad,
That nosey thieving little louse,
Comes sneaking in your empty house.
She looks around. She quickly notes
Three bowls brimful of porridge oats.
And while still standing on her feet,
She grabs a spoon and starts to eat.
I say again, how *would* you feel
If you had made this lovely meal
And some delinquent little tot
Broke in and gobbled up the lot?
But wait! That's not the worst of it!
Now comes the most distressing bit.
You are of course a houseproud wife,

And all your happy married life
You have collected lovely things
Like gilded cherubs wearing wings,
And furniture by Chippendale
Bought at some famous auction sale.
But your most special valued treasure,

The piece that gives you endless pleasure,

Is one small children's dining-chair,

Elizabethan, very rare.

It is in fact your joy and pride,

Passed down to you on grandma's side.

But Goldilocks, like many freaks,

Does not appreciate antiques.

She doesn't care, she doesn't mind,

And now she plonks her fat behind
Upon this dainty precious chair,
And crunch! It busts beyond repair.
A nice girl would at once exclaim,
"Oh dear! Oh heavens! What a shame!"
Not Goldie. She begins to swear.
She bellows, "What a lousy chair!"

And uses *one* disgusting word
That luckily you've never heard.
(I dare not write it, even hint it.
Nobody would ever print it.)

You'd think by now this little skunk
Would have the sense to do a bunk.
But no. I very much regret
She hasn't nearly finished yet.
Deciding she would like a rest,
She says, "Let's see which bed is best."
Upstairs she goes and tries all three.
(Here comes the next catastrophe.)
Most educated people choose
To rid themselves of socks and shoes
Before they clamber into bed.
But Goldie didn't give a shred.
Her filthy shoes were thick with grime,
And mud and mush and slush and slime.
Worse still, upon the heel of one
Was something that a dog had done.
I say once more, what *would* you think
If all this horrid dirt and stink
Was smeared upon your eiderdown
By this revolting little clown?
(The famous story has no clues
To show the girl removed her shoes.)
Oh, what a tale of crime on crime!
Let's check it for a second time.

CRIME ONE, THE PROSECUTION'S CASE:
SHE BREAKS AND ENTERS SOMEONE'S PLACE.

CRIME TWO, THE PROSECUTOR NOTES:
SHE STEALS A BOWL OF PORRIDGE OATS.

CRIME THREE: SHE BREAKS A PRECIOUS CHAIR
BELONGING TO THE BABY BEAR.

CRIME FOUR: SHE SMEARS EACH SPOTLESS SHEET
WITH FILTHY MESSES FROM HER FEET.

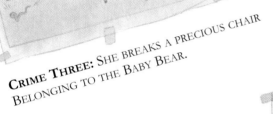

A judge would say without a blink,
"Ten years hard labour in the clink!"
But in the book, as you will see,
The little beast gets off scot-free,
While tiny children near and far

Shout, "Goody-goody! Hooray! Hurrah!"
"Poor darling Goldilocks!" they say,
"Thank goodness that she got away!"

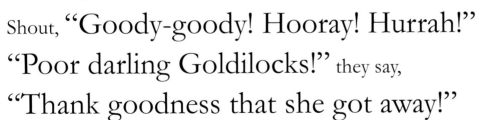

Myself, I think I'd rather send
Young Goldie to a sticky end.

"Oh daddy!" cried the Baby Bear,

"My porridge gone! It isn't fair!"

"Then go upstairs," the Big Bear said,

"Your porridge is upon the bed.

"But as it's inside mademoiselle,

"You'll have to

eat her up as well."

The Cremation of

By Robert Service

"Cold (very cold) and hot (very hot) is what this utterly creepy tale is all about. Told with deceptively crude slang and pounding rhythms, it pulls you along like the long sleigh ride it is, and then dumps you out so you can cringe and grin. If ever there was a campfire yarn, this is it. Just keep your eye on the fire!"

AVI

Sam McGee

There are strange things done in the midnight sun
By the men who moil for gold;
The Arctic trails have their secret tales
That would make your blood run cold;
The Northern Lights have seen queer sights,
But the queerest they ever did see
Was that night on the marge of Lake Lebarge
I cremated Sam McGee.

Now Sam McGee was from Tennessee, where the cotton
      blooms and blows.
Why he left his home in the South to roam round the Pole
      God only knows.
He was always cold, but the land of gold seemed to hold him
      like a spell;
Though he'd often say in his homely way that he'd "sooner
      live in hell."
On a Christmas Day we were mushing our way over the
      Dawson trail.
Talk of your cold! through the parka's fold it stabbed like a
      driven nail.
If our eyes we'd close, then the lashes froze, till sometimes we
      couldn't see;
It wasn't much fun, but the only one to whimper was Sam
      McGee.

And that very night as we lay packed tight in our robes beneath
      the snow,
And the dogs were fed, and the stars o'erhead were dancing
      heel and toe,
He turned to me, and, "Cap," says he, "I'll cash in this trip,
      I guess;
And if I do, I'm asking that you won't refuse my last request."

Well, he seemed so low that I couldn't say no: then he says
      with a sort of moan:

"It's the cursèd cold, and it's got right hold till I'm chilled
    clean through to the bone.
Yet 'taint being dead, it's my awful dread of the icy grave that
        pains:
So I want you to swear that, foul or fair, you'll cremate my
    last remains."

A pal's last need is a thing to heed, so I swore I would not fail;
And we started on at the streak of dawn, but God! he looked
        ghastly pale.
He crouched on the sleigh, and he raved all day of his home
    in Tennessee;
And before nightfall a corpse was all that was left of Sam
        McGee.

There wasn't a breath in that land of death, and I hurried, horror driven,
    With a corpse half-hid that I couldn't get rid because of a promise given;
It was lashed to the sleigh, and it seemed to say: "You may tax your brawn and brains,
    But you promised true, and it's up to you to cremate those last remains."

Now a promise made is a debt unpaid, and the trail has its own stern code.
In the days to come, though my lips were dumb, in my heart how I cursed that load.
In the long, long night, by the lone firelight, while the huskies, round in a ring,
Howled out their woes to the homeless snows—O God! how I loathed the thing!

And every day that quiet clay seemed to heavy and heavier grow;
And on I went, though the dogs were spent and the grub was getting low;
The trail was bad, and I felt half mad, but I swore I would not give in;
And I'd often sing to the hateful thing, and it hearkened with a grin.

Till I came to the marge of Lake Lebarge, and a derelict there lay;

It was jammed in the ice, but I saw in a trice it was called
      the "Alice May."
And I looked at it, and I thought a bit, and I looked at my
      frozen chum:
Then, "Here," said I, with a sudden cry, "is my cre-ma-tor-eum."

Some planks I tore from the cabin floor, and I lit the boiler
      fire;
Some coal I found that was lying around, and I heaped
      the fuel higher;
The flames just soared, and the furnace roared—such a
      blaze you seldom see;
And I burrowed a hole in the glowing coal, and I stuffed
      in Sam McGee.

Then I made a hike, for I didn't like to hear him sizzle so;
And the heavens scowled, and the huskies howled, and the
      wind began to blow.

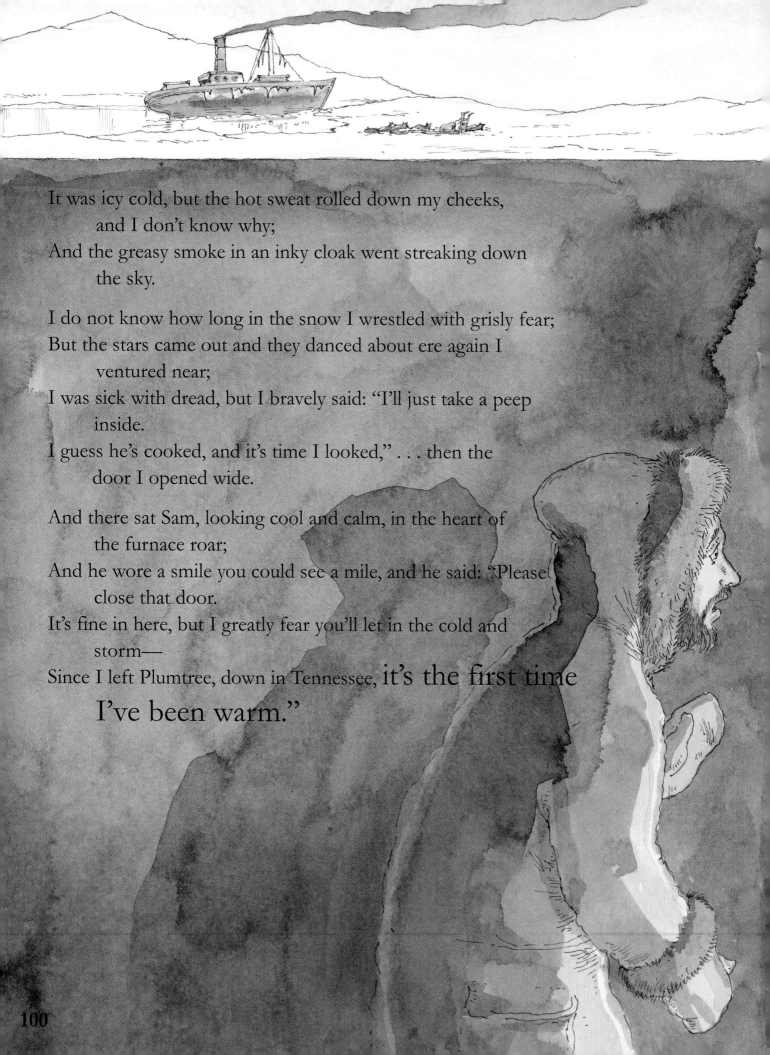

It was icy cold, but the hot sweat rolled down my cheeks,
 and I don't know why;
And the greasy smoke in an inky cloak went streaking down
 the sky.

I do not know how long in the snow I wrestled with grisly fear;
But the stars came out and they danced about ere again I
 ventured near;
I was sick with dread, but I bravely said: "I'll just take a peep
 inside.
I guess he's cooked, and it's time I looked," . . . then the
 door I opened wide.

And there sat Sam, looking cool and calm, in the heart of
 the furnace roar;
And he wore a smile you could see a mile, and he said: "Please
 close that door.
It's fine in here, but I greatly fear you'll let in the cold and
 storm—
Since I left Plumtree, down in Tennessee, it's the first time
 I've been warm."

There are strange things done in the midnight sun
By the men who moil for gold;
The Arctic trails have their secret tales
That would make your blood run cold.
The Northern Lights have seen queer sights,
But the queerest they ever did see
Was that night on the marge of Lake Lebarge
I cremated Sam McGee.

O What is That

By W. H. Auden

"In this age-old story of war, dread and fear, there is a relentless drumbeat—the tramp of marching feet—with every verse coming closer. This poem with its sense of impending horror asks us to imagine the terror of conflict in our country, our town, on our street. . . ."

MICHAEL MORPURGO

Sound

O what is that sound which so thrills the ear
  Down in the valley drumming, drumming?
Only the scarlet soldiers, dear,
  The soldiers coming.

O what is that light I see flashing so clear
　　Over the distance brightly, brightly?
Only the sun on their weapons, dear,
　　　As they step lightly.

O what are they doing with all that gear,
　　What are they doing this morning, this morning?
Only their usual manoeuvres, dear,
　　　Or perhaps a warning.

O why have they left the road down there,
　　Why are they suddenly wheeling, wheeling?
Perhaps a change in their orders, dear.
　　　Why are you kneeling?

O haven't they stopped for the doctor's care,
　　Haven't they reined their horses, their horses?
Why, they are none of them wounded, dear,
　　　None of these forces.

O is it the parson they want, with white hair,
　　Is it the parson, is it, is it?
No, they are passing his gateway, dear,
　　　Without a visit.

O it must be the farmer who lives so near.
     It must be the farmer so cunning, so cunning?
They have passed the farmyard already, dear,
          And now they are running.

O where are you going? Stay with me here!
     Were the vows you swore deceiving, deceiving?
No, I promised to love you, dear,
          But I must be leaving.

O it's broken the lock and splintered the door,
     O it's the gate where they're turning, turning;
Their boots are heavy on the floor
          And their eyes are burning.

The Owl and the

By Edward Lear

"I've always thought the Owl and the Pussy-cat were the most wonderfully romantic alternative couple. I've often wondered if they had children. How lovely to find out about the feathery brothers and furry sisters in the little-known sequel!"

JACQUELINE WILSON

Pussy-cat

The Owl and the Pussy-cat went to sea
In a beautiful pea-green boat,
They took some honey, and plenty of money,
Wrapped up in a five-pound note.
The Owl looked up to the stars above,
And sang to a small guitar,
"O lovely Pussy! O Pussy, my love
What a beautiful Pussy you are,
You are,
You are!
What a beautiful Pussy you are!"

Pussy said to the Owl, "You elegant fowl!

How charmingly sweet you sing!

O let us be married! Too long we have tarried:

But what shall we do for a ring?"

They sailed away, for a year and a day,

To the land where the Bong-tree grows,

And there in a wood a Piggy-wig stood

With a ring at the end of his nose,

His nose,

His nose,

With a ring at the end of his nose.

"Dear Pig, are you willing to sell for one shilling
    Your ring?" Said the Piggy, "I will."
So they took it away, and were married next day
    By the Turkey who lives on the hill.
They dined on mince, and slices of quince,
    Which they ate with a runcible spoon;
And hand in hand, on the edge of the sand,
    They danced by the light of the moon,
        The moon,
            The moon,
    They danced by the light of the moon.

from The Children of the

By Edward Lear

Our mother was the Pussy-cat, our father was the Owl,

And so we're partly little beasts and partly little fowl,

The brothers of our family have feathers and they hoot,

While all the sisters dress in fur and have long tails to boot.

We all believe that **little mice,**

For food are **singularly nice.**

Owl and the Pussy-cat

Our mother died long years ago. She was a lovely cat

    Her tail was 5 feet long, and grey with stripes, but what of that?

In Sila forest on the East of far Calabria's shore

    She tumbled from a lofty tree—none ever saw her more.

Our owly father long was ill from sorrow and surprise,

    But with the feathers of his tail he wiped his weeping eyes.

And in the hollow of a tree in Sila's inmost maze

    We made a happy home and there we pass our obvious days.

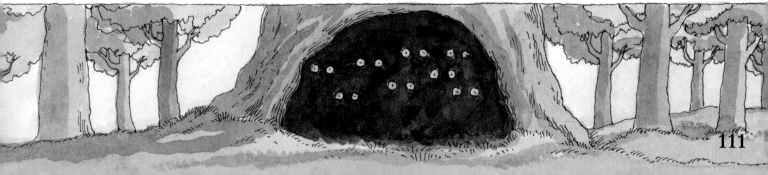

Wynken, Blynken,

By Eugene Field

"There's no journey more sublime
than that taken by Wynken, Blynken, and
Nod. The lullaby quality of Field's
poetry will rock anyone—child or adult—
into a sweet, twinkling sleep."
MARY POPE OSBORNE

and Nod

Wynken, Blynken, and Nod one night
   Sailed off in a wooden shoe—
Sailed on a river of crystal light,
   Into a sea of dew.
"Where are you going and what do you wish?"
   The old moon asked the three.
"We have come to fish for the herring-fish
   That live in this beautiful sea;
Nets of silver and gold have we,"
   Said Wynken, Blynken, and Nod.

The old moon laughed and sang a song,
As they rocked in the wooden shoe,
And the wind that sped them all night long
Ruffled the waves of dew.
The little stars were the herring-fish
That lived in that beautiful sea—
"Now cast your nets wherever you wish—
But never afeared are we";
So cried the stars to the fishermen three:
Wynken, Blynken, and Nod.

All night long their nets they threw
To the stars in the twinkling foam—
Then down from the skies came the wooden shoe,
Bringing the fishermen home;
'Twas all so pretty a sail, it seemed
As if it could not be,
And some folks thought 'twas a dream they'd dreamed
Of sailing that beautiful sea—
But I shall name you the fishermen three:
Wynken, Blynken, and Nod.

Wynken and Blynken are two little eyes,
    And Nod is a little head,
And the wooden shoe that sailed the skies
    Is a wee one's trundle-bed.
So shut your eyes while mother sings
    Of wonderful sights that be,
And you shall see the beautiful things
    As you rock on the misty sea,
Where the old shoe rocked the fishermen three:

Wynken, Blynken, and Nod.

Afterword

What wonders! What word-journeys!

And then there's the kind of poem that doesn't exactly tell a story but hints at all the stories it could tell. Poems that could "play football and get picked for England," poems about secrets, poems about precious memories.

That's how this anthology begins, with a punch of a poem by Roger McGough; and how it ends, with six simple, heart-wrenching lines by the American poet, Langston Hughes. "Oh! All I could have told you," he seems to say. "My friend and I, our friendship was as wide and deep as the world…"

There are so many ways of telling stories. Just imagine!

Kevin Crossley-Holland

Poem

I loved my friend.
He went away from me.
There's nothing more to say.
The poem ends,
Soft as it began—
I loved my friend.

By Langston Hughes

About the Artists

Peter and Siân Bailey are married and live in Birkenhead, England.

Peter Bailey has illustrated books by many well-known children's authors, including Philip Pullman, Allan Ahlberg, Joan Aiken, and Adele Geras. He particularly admires the work of Brian Robb, Edward Ardizzone, and Quentin Blake, all of whom, it seems to him, use drawing as a special kind of "handwriting." Peter works mostly in pen line and washes over the line with watercolor.

Siân is a painter who loves all things mythical and magical. Her precise and beautiful style echoes the images found in illuminated manuscripts and is perfect for the legendary poems included in this collection. Her early influences were the Pre-Raphaelite painters and also the Florentine frescos. Siân works with very fine brushes in gouache and sometimes watercolor.

Peter and Siân both work at home—Siân in a tiny room crammed with books, Peter sitting at the kitchen table.

Carol Lawson and Chris McEwan are married and live in Sussex, England.

Carol Lawson's attention to detail and love of color comes from her great interest in the Pre-Raphaelites. Her distinctive style has evolved from working in minute detail using specially mixed watercolors to experimenting with color and texture using gouache and acrylics. Carol loves the challenge of working on a wide variety of subjects, as demonstrated by the poems she has illustrated in this book.

Chris McEwan comes from an artistic family. After leaving art college, he worked in Paris as a fashion illustrator and has never lost his love of costume. It was there that Chris was first introduced to the work of American artist Winsor McCay, whose cartoon creations have become a major influence on his work. In addition to illustrating books, Chris has worked in animation. He also collects toys, in particular, robots, and works surrounded by all the things you can find in his pictures.

Carol and Chris share a studio in their home. Carol normally has Teddy, their cat, asleep on her lap while she works.

All four artists met at Brighton Art College, England.

About the Writers

Jim Who Ran Away from his Nurse, and Was Eaten by a Lion

Hilaire Belloc (1870–1953) was born in France and became a British subject in 1902. He was an active politician, a newspaper journalist, editor, and novelist. But he is most widely known for his nonsense poems, which make fun of the behavior and manners of the time. His cautionary tales like *Jim* and *Matilda Told Such Dreadful Lies* poke fun at Victorian stories, in which children's disobedience brought them terrible ill fortune.

J. K. Rowling (1965–) was born in England and wrote her first story when she was five, about a rabbit who got the measles! She became an extremely successful children's writer when her first novel, *Harry Potter and the Sorcerer's Stone*, was published in 1997. Before this, Joanne Kathleen Rowling worked as a secretary, taught English in Portugal, and then moved to Scotland to finish her first book about Harry Potter. There are now five titles in the seven-book series. By 2003, 192 million copies had been sold in over 200 countries, and the books have been translated into at least 55 languages, including Latin! The first two books have been made into hugely popular films.

Paul Revere's Ride

Henry Wadsworth Longfellow (1807–1882) was born in Portland, Maine, and is probably best known for the epic poem *Hiawatha*. He was among the first American poets to write about the people, landscapes, and themes of his homeland. Paul Revere was a real historical figure and was involved in the American War of Independence 1775–1781. Longfellow taught and he travelled widely, living for many years in Cambridge, England, where he was known for his long hair, flowered waistcoats, and yellow gloves!

Sharon Creech (1945–) was born in Ohio, and is a writer of novels for adults and children. She uses memories of her own childhood as inspiration for her family stories. Sharon Creech's best-loved children's novels include the winner of the Newbery Medal, *Walk Two Moons*, and *Love That Dog*. In 2002, she became the first American to win the CILIP Carnegie Medal, with *Ruby Holler*.

Jabberwocky

Lewis Carroll (1832–1898) was born in England. His real name was C. L. Dodgson and he lectured in mathematics at Oxford University. He took holy orders in 1861 and became a priest. Carroll was a shy person who preferred the company of children, using them as inspiration for his writing, drawing, and photography. His most famous work, *Alice's Adventures in Wonderland*, was written for Alice Liddell, the daughter of the Dean of Christ Church College, Oxford. *Jabberwocky* is taken from the sequel, *Through the Looking-Glass,* and was first published in 1871.

Philip Pullman (1946–) was born in England but spent his early childhood in different parts of the world. He began writing for children when he was a teacher, basing some of his novels on plays he wrote for his pupils, such as *The Ruby in the Smoke*. He gained enormous popularity with the publication of his children's trilogy, *His Dark Materials*. The first book in the trilogy, *Northern Lights*, went on to win the Carnegie Medal in 1996. The final part, *The Amber Spyglass*, became the first children's book to win the Whitbread Book of the Year in 2001. Philip Pullman was made a CBE in the 2004 New Year's Honors List and *His Dark Materials* was voted number three in the 2003 BBC Big Read.

Merlin and the Snake's Egg

Leslie Norris (1921–) was born in Wales but now lives in the U.S.A. He has written poetry since he was twenty, as well as working as a teacher and a headmaster. More recently he has taught creative writing and literature at a variety of universities in America. He has published eleven collections of poems.

Kevin Crossley-Holland (1941–) was born in England and is a poet and translator. He is also famous for his retellings of traditional tales for children. He has won critical acclaim for his Arthur trilogy for children. *The Seeing Stone*, the first book in the trilogy, won the 2001 Guardian Children's Fiction Award. Kevin Crossley-Holland's novella, *Storm*, won the 1985 Carnegie Medal.

The Man From Snowy River

A. B. "Banjo" Paterson (1864–1941) was born near Orange in New South Wales, Australia. He worked as a solicitor and a war correspondent. After *The Man From Snowy River and Other Verses* was published in 1895, he was hailed as a literary representative of Australia. He also wrote the unofficial national anthem of Australia, "Waltzing Matilda."

Morris Gleitzman (1953–) was born in England and moved to Australia when he was sixteen. Before becoming a children's author he was, among other things, a frozen-chicken thawer, a department-store Santa, a fashion-industry trainee, a TV producer, and a screenwriter! His highly successful books, which include *The Other Facts of Life, Two Weeks With the Queen, Bumface,* and *Teacher's Pet,* have won many awards and have been published internationally. In 1999, he was voted Favorite Australian Author in the Dymocks Booksellers' Children's Choice Awards.

A Visit from St. Nicholas

Clement Clarke Moore (1779–1863) was born into a wealthy American family in New York and inherited farmland that became the city's Chelsea District. He was a biblical scholar, teacher, and poet. Tradition has it that Moore was on his way to buy turkeys for the poor on Christmas Eve, 1822, when he was inspired to write *A Visit from St. Nicholas* as a surprise for his family. It was first published anonymously in 1823.

David Almond (1951–) was born in England. He's been a hotel porter, a laborer, and a teacher. He gave up his teaching job, sold his house, and went to live in a commune in order to become a full-time writer. He published his first novel for children, *Skellig,* to great acclaim, winning the 1998 Whitbread Children's Book Award and the 1998 Carnegie Medal. His novel, *The Fire-Eaters,* won the 2003 Nestlé Smarties Book Prize Gold Medal and the 2003 Whitbread Children's Book of the Year Award.

Brave Boy Rap

Tony Mitton (1951–) was born in North Africa. His father was a soldier and he spent his childhood in Africa, Hong Kong, and Germany. After studying English at Cambridge University, he became an elementary school teacher. Mitton now writes poems and stories full-time and won great acclaim for *Plum,* and a Silver Medal at the 2000 Nestlé Smarties Book Prize for *The Red and White Spotted Handkerchief.*

Philip Ardagh (1961–) was born in Kent, England. He was an advertising copywriter, a hospital cleaner, and a reader-for-the-blind before writing more than sixty books. He is most widely known for his best-selling Eddie Dickens trilogy, *Awful Ends, Dreadful Acts,* and *Terrible Times,* which has been translated into twenty-six languages and is being developed for a series of films by Warner Bros. He is currently writing a children's book with Paul McCartney. And, oh yes, he's very tall and very bearded!

The Grateful Dragon

Raymond Wilson (1925–1995) was born and lived in Britain. He worked in the field of education as a schoolteacher and university professor. Poetry was his great joy and, during his lifetime, he edited several anthologies both for young and older children. Wilson's own poems have been broadcast and published over a period of forty years.

Eva Ibbotson (1925–) was born in Vienna, Austria. She wrote her very first stories in German, but began writing in English when her family emigrated to Britain. Eva Ibbotson was over forty before she wrote her first full-length novel—the children's book *The Great Ghost Rescue.* She has since alternated between writing for adults and children, and is a firm favorite with both. Many of her children's books are ghost stories—even though she admits to being terrified of them as a child! In 2001, her novel, *Journey to the River Sea,* was awarded the Nestlé Smarties Book Prize Gold Medal.

The Highwayman

Alfred Noyes (1880–1958) was British and published his first volume of poetry, *The Loom Years*, when he was just twenty-one. It is thought that *The Highwayman* is a romanticized account of Dick Turpin, the eighteenth-century English outlaw. Noyes was Professor of English Literature at Princeton University, but he returned to Britain in 1949.

Cornelia Funke (1958–) is one of Germany's most successful children's authors and has written more than forty books. Cornelia has had great international success with her novels, *The Thief Lord* and *Inkheart*, and both of these have been *New York Times* bestsellers. *The Thief Lord* won the Book Sense Book of the Year Award 2002, the Swiss Youth Literature Award, and the Mildred L. Batchelder Award for Best Translated Book, among many other accolades.

The Late Passenger

C. S. Lewis (1898–1963) came from Northern Ireland but moved to England, where he taught at both Oxford and Cambridge Universities. While in Oxford he regularly met with other writers – among them J. R. R. Tolkien, the author of *The Lord of the Rings* – to discuss their work. The main focus of his writing was his conversion to Christianity. Young readers know him best for *The Lion, the Witch, and the Wardrobe* and other titles in the *Chronicles of Narnia* series.

G. P. Taylor (1960–) was born in England. He is now the vicar of Cloughton in Yorkshire but his career has covered many areas, including working in the music industry and being a policeman. Taylor published the first edition of his novel, *Shadowmancer*, himself, raising the money by selling his motorcycle. *Shadowmancer* has since been taken on by Faber & Faber and has become a best-seller, with more than a quarter of a million copies sold. G. P. Taylor now divides his time between writing and working in his parish.

Goldilocks and the Three Bears

Roald Dahl (1916–1990) was born in Wales to Norwegian parents and was educated at a variety of English boarding schools. He began writing professionally during the Second World War with a story based on his experience in the RAF. Dahl went on to write some of the most successful novels and poetry ever written for children, including *Charlie and the Chocolate Factory*, *Matilda*, and *Revolting Rhymes* – from which *Goldilocks and the Three Bears* is taken. Asked how he was able to write such successful books for children he replied, "It's because *I am* eight years old."

Eoin Colfer (1965–) was born and lives in Ireland. He was a teacher before he became a writer, having enjoyed telling gory stories to his pupils. Eoin still regards teaching as his first love. He had written five novels before *Artemis Fowl* was published, but it is the excitement surrounding this particular book that established Eoin Colfer as one of the biggest new names in children's fiction. It was shortlisted for the 2001 Whitbread Children's Book of the Year and won the 2002 WH Smith Award, Children's Category. A film is currently being made. The second book in the trilogy, *Artemis Fowl: The Arctic Incident*, became a number-one bestseller in 2002.

The Cremation of Sam McGee

Robert Service (1874–1958) was born in Preston in England to Scottish parents and was educated at the University of Glasgow. He emigrated to Canada in 1897 and, from there, led a vagabond existence as he traveled down through the U.S.A. to Mexico before moving to France. His travels inspired his ballads and novels and he became a very successful author. He was often referred to as "the Canadian Kipling."

Avi (1937–) is a popular and versatile American children's author who began his career as a playwright. His twin sister gave him the name Avi when they were very young and he has not used another name since. His best-loved novels include *The Fighting Ground* and *Blue Heron*. He won the 2003 Newbery Medal for his 50th novel, *Crispin: The Cross of Lead*, and it became a *New York Times* best-seller.

O What is That Sound

W. H. Auden (1907–1973) was born in England and is considered to be one of the twentieth century's greatest poets. He travelled in Germany, Iceland, and China, and served in the Spanish Civil War before settling in the U.S.A. and becoming an American citizen. Auden was able to write many different forms of poetry. Political ballads of the past were the main influences on *O What is That Sound* In 1948, Auden won the Pulitzer Prize for poetry. His work has had a major influence on succeeding generations of poets on both sides of the Atlantic.

Michael Morpurgo (1943–) was born in England. He has a great reputation in the world of British children's books and was made Children's Laureate 2003–2005. He has written more than ninety books, both novels and picture books. Michael won the 1995 Whitbread Children's Book Award for *Wreck of the Zanzibar* and the 1996 Nestlé Smarties Book Prize with *The Butterfly Lion*. He and his wife devote much of their time to their charity, Farms for City Children.

The Owl and the Pussy-cat and The Children of the Owl and the Pussy-cat

Edward Lear (1812–1888) was born in England and was the second youngest in a family of twenty-one children. His main job was as an artist and in 1846 he gave drawing lessons to Queen Victoria. Lear first created nonsense verse and limericks to entertain the Earl of Derby's children and delighted in being known as "The Father of Nonsense." Lear was living in Cannes in France when he composed *The Owl and the Pussy-cat* for a young child who was sick in bed. The incomplete poem, *The Children of the Owl and the Pussy-cat,* was found after his death on the yellow inside cover of a book that Lear used as a journal. He told the whole story in a letter to a child friend of his, but sadly never finished the poem.

Jacqueline Wilson (1945–) was born in England and wrote her first "novel" in a Woolworth's exercise book when she was nine. She has since sold more than fifteen million children's books in the UK alone and in 2003 more of her books were borrowed from UK libraries than any other author. Her novel, *The Illustrated Mum*, won the 2000 Blue Peter People's Choice Award and the 1999 Guardian Children's Fiction Award.

Wynken, Blynken, and Nod

Eugene Field (1850–1895) was brought up in Massachusetts. He was nine when he wrote his first poem, about Fido the farm dog. He worked as a journalist, writing a humorous column "Sharps and Flats" in the *Chicago Daily News*. Field was nicknamed "The Children's Poet" because he only wrote poems for young readers. *Wynken, Blynken, and Nod* is one of his most famous rhymes. Another is *Little Boy Blue*.

Mary Pope Osborne (1949–) was born in Fort Sill, Oklahoma. The daughter of an army colonel, she loved the excitement of moving frequently from place to place with her family. The constant change of scenery fuelled her imagination. As a teenager, Mary continued to explore new and imaginary worlds by becoming deeply involved in the theater. After college and traveling around Europe and Asia, she married an actor and moved to New York City. One day, on the roof of her apartment building, she began writing a story that became the popular young adult novel *Run, Run, Fast as You Can*. Mary Pope Osborne has since written more than sixty children's books—including *Favorite Greek Myths*, *Favorite Medieval Tales*, *Adaline Falling Star*, *Rocking Horse Christmas*, and several books in the Dear America series. She is best known as the author of the Magic Tree House series, which has sold more than twenty-five million copies and is published in twenty-one countries.

A Good Poem

Roger McGough (1937–) grew up in Liverpool, England, during the Second World War. He made his name as one of the Mersey Poets alongside Brian Patten and Adrian Henri. McGough's first collection of poems for children was published in 1976. Having worked as a teacher and lecturer, he has an ongoing commitment to getting poetry into schools. He has also won two BAFTAs for his writing for film, and in 1997 was awarded the OBE for his work.

Poem

Langston Hughes (1902–1967) was born in Joplin, Missouri, and educated at Columbia University. He traveled widely as a sailor on a freighter, before jumping ship and taking work as a cook and doorman in a Parisian nightclub. *The Weary Blues*, his first volume of poetry, was published in 1926 and secured Hughes' reputation as the Harlem Renaissance's most prominent black writer. His poetry is deeply influenced by jazz and the blues.

Sources & Acknowledgements

W. H. Auden: "O What is That Sound" from *Collected Shorter Poems 1927–1957* (Faber & Faber, 1969), © W. H. Auden, reprinted by permission of Faber & Faber Ltd and Random House Inc.

Hilaire Belloc: "Jim Who Ran Away from his Nurse, and Was Eaten by a Lion" from *Cautionary Verses* (Duckworth), © 1970, The Estate of Hilaire Belloc, reprinted by permission of Peters Fraser & Dunlop Group on behalf of The Estate of Hilaire Belloc.

Roald Dahl: "Goldilocks and the Three Bears" from *Revolting Rhymes* (Jonathan Cape, 1982), text © Roald Dahl Nominee Ltd, 1982, reprinted by permission of David Higham Associates and Alfred A. Knopf, an imprint of Random House Children's Books, a division of Random House Inc.

Langston Hughes: "Poem" from *The Collected Poems of Langston Hughes* (Knopf, 1994), © 1994 by The Estate of Langston Hughes, reprinted by permission of Alfred A. Knopf, a division of Random House, Inc., and David Higham Associates.

C. S. Lewis: "The Late Passenger" from *The Collected Poems of C. S. Lewis*, edited by Walter Hooper (Fount/HarperCollins Publishers, 1994), © C. S. Lewis Pte Ltd, 1964, reprinted by permission of the C. S. Lewis Company Ltd.

Roger McGough: "A Good Poem" from *In the Glassroom* (Jonathan Cape, 1976), © 1976, Roger McGough, reprinted by permission of Peters Fraser & Dunlop Group on behalf of Roger McGough.

Tony Mitton: "Brave Boy Rap" from *Groovy Greek Hero Raps* (Orchard Books, 2001), reprinted by permission of David Higham Associates.

Leslie Norris: "Merlin and the Snake's Egg" from *Merlin and the Snake's Egg* (New York: The Viking Press, 1978), reprinted by permission of the author.

Alfred Noyes: "The Highwayman" [Part I & Part II] from *The Highwayman* (Oxford University Press, 1981), reprinted by permission of David Higham Associates.

Robert Service: "The Cremation of Sam McGee" from *The Best of Robert Service* A & C Black, 1995), 1907 Dodd, Mead & Co, New York, British Reversionary rights licensed by the Estate of Robert Service c/o M. Wm Krasilovsky (Agent), 51 East 42nd Street, New York, NY 10017.

Raymond Wilson: "The Grateful Dragon" from *Dragon Poems* (Oxford University Press, 1991), reprinted by permission of Mrs G. M. Wilson.

Every effort has been made to contact all copyright holders. The publishers would be pleased to rectify any omissions brought to their notice at the earliest opportunity.